Pekoe

Written by Candace L. Newland

Illustratrated by Suzanne Kinstle Nocera

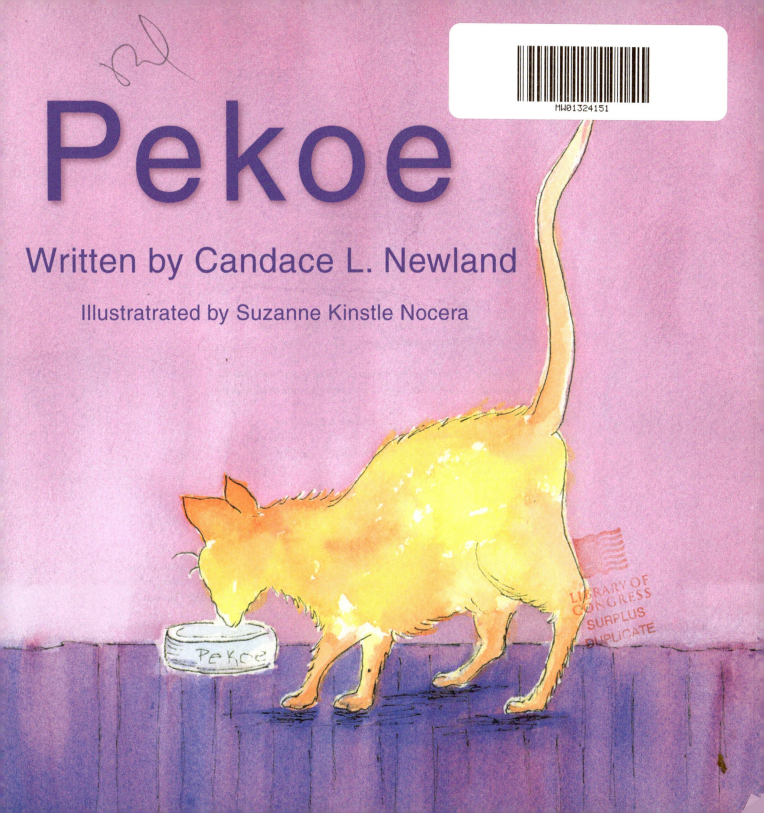

AuthorHouse™ LLC
1663 Liberty Drive
Bloomington, IN 47403
www.authorhouse.com
Phone: 1-800-839-8640

© 2014 Candace L. Newland. All Rights Reserved.
Illustratrated by Suzanne Kinstle Nocera

No part of this book may be reproduced, stored in a retrieval system,
or transmitted by any means without the written permission of the author.

Published by AuthorHouse 02/25/2014

ISBN: 978-1-4918-2893-9 (sc)

Library of Congress Control Number: 2014903603

This book is printed on acid-free paper.

Because of the dynamic nature of the Internet, any web addresses or links contained in this book may have changed since publication and may no longer be valid. The views expressed in this work are solely those of the author and do not necessarily reflect the views of the publisher, and the publisher hereby disclaims any responsibility for them.

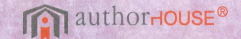

In memory of Nelda who found me and Maggie who taught me.

It is so cold here in the woods. I don't even know how I got here. One minute I was riding in a warm car and the next minute I was tossed into these cold dark woods. It is so scary here. Surely someone will come looking for me.

Shhh. I hear a voice. "Here kitty, kitty, kitty". I'm not too sure about this person. I don't know her but I'm very hungry and I smell some food. Maybe just one bite and I'll run away.

This tastes so good. She has a nice voice. She seems very friendly. Now she's petting me. Well, that's not so bad. In fact, this is very nice.

The soft voiced lady picks me up and takes me into her kitchen. "I'd like to keep you but I already have two cats and I just don't have room for another" she says. "But I know someone who just might want to adopt a kitten as cute as you."

Soon I hear another woman talking. "Of course we'll adopt him. He can be an indoor cat. I'm sure our dogs Maggie and Cody will like him. I'll make an appointment with the veterinarian to make sure he is healthy and that he will be able to have a good life even though he does have this disability."

The next day the lady takes me to the veterinarian. "Other than his obvious challenges, he is perfectly healthy" she says. "I'm so glad that you are willing to give him a home. He really will be able to adjust and live a very normal life."

"We are going to name him Pekoe because he is orange and his purring is as comforting as a cup of tea." says my new lady. It sounds like a good name to me.

Disability? I can't imagine what disability I have. What could it be? Is it something bad? Is it something I'm missing? I guess I'll have to check with my new friends Maggie and Cody to see what a disability is.

Maggie is a very tall golden retriever. Maybe being short is my disability. But no, I don't think so. I'm almost as tall as Cody, the Sheltie, and nobody says he has a disability. No, being short isn't a disability.

Ahhh—maybe it's having a small nose. Maggie's is big and black but Cody's is quite small. I can sniff at treats just like they do. I can smell my dinner just like they do. No, having a small nose isn't a disability.

Bang! Bang! Bang! There's a clue! Maggie's tail is long and very strong. It makes quite a bang when she hits furniture with it. But my tail is very lovely too. It stands up tall as I walk along and it is much longer than Cody's. No, my tail is just right for me. It isn't my disability.

Hey, here's a possibility. Big ears! But if ears are only used for hearing, mine are just fine. I can hear the birds outside singing. I can hear my people open a can of my dinner from clear upstairs. I can hear the wind swishing through the trees outside the screen door. Maggie's ears are much bigger than mine but Cody's are just a little taller than mine. No, my small ears are not my disability.

There is the vacuum cleaner again. My people are always complaining about all the dog hair and say they need to vacuum again. Could it be that my disability is that I don't shed enough hair? I thought that I was leaving plenty on the back of the couch and just yesterday, my lady said that I was getting hair all over her coat. No, something else must be my disability.

Woof! Woof! Yipe! Yipe! There they go again, barking at the neighbor's cat. Cody even barks at the neighbor's car. Silly dogs! Could it be that my quiet "Purrrr" is my disability? Well, I can do more than Purrrr. Yowl! Yowl! Wow, was that ever a great noise! That was almost as loud as Maggie's bark. No, I don't think that my voice is my disability.

Squish, squish, squish. Here comes Maggie in from the rain. I could almost drown in the puddles her big paws leave on the floor. My paws are so tiny compared to hers but Cody has much smaller paws. In fact, mine are almost the same size as his. No, small paws are not my disability.

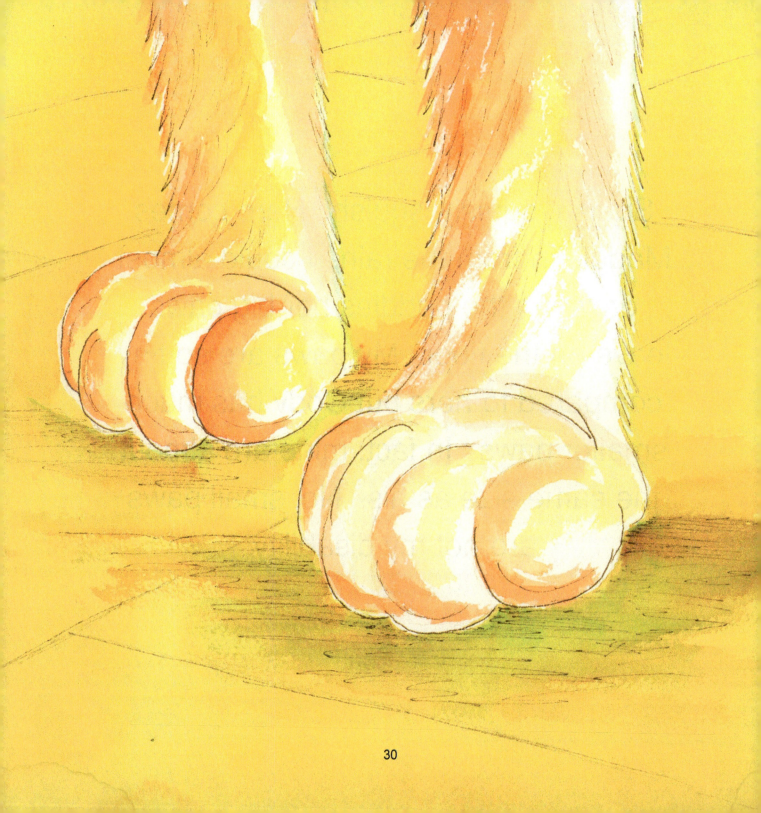

Here comes Maggie across the kitchen floor. She has long toenails that tap, tap, tap when she walks. Cody's toenails don't make as much noise and his are so much smaller. Well, that could be my disability. Mine don't make any noise at all. But, if I made noise when I walked, how could I sneak up on a fly? No, having quiet feet is not my disability.

Maybe my disability is something that I can't do that my friends can. I guess I'll just have to ask them. I can't imagine that they can do anything that I can't if I set my mind to it. In fact, I can do lots of things that they can't. I can climb the tree in the sunroom.

I can hide under the couch.

I can crawl into the clothes dryer and sleep in the clothes basket.

I can walk on the countertops—until my people catch me! Why what could I possibly be missing?

Here come Maggie and Cody. They will tell me what a disability is.

Hi Maggie. Hi Cody. I am supposed to have a disability but I just don't know what it is. Is a disability bad? Should I try to lose it?

"Well, Pekoe," says Maggie, "a disability is something that makes life more challenging for you. Your disability is that you cannot see. You are blind. I recognized it right away because, before I came to live here, I was a seeing eye dog. That means that I led the way for a girl who was blind so I know all about it."

WOW! Blind! I would have never guessed that was my disability. I'm so glad it's not something important that I'm missing. A disability isn't such a bad thing to have after all. It just makes my life more challenging and challenges are a good thing! Now, I hear a fly buzzing in the sunroom that I need to catch.

CPSIA information can be obtained at www.ICGtesting.com
Printed in the USA
BVOW10s2047110314

347367BV00002B/19/P